www.tredition.de

AF177293

May Woodham

You Are Immortal

Poems

www.tredition.de

© 2018 May Woodham

Verlag und Druck: tredition GmbH, Hamburg

ISBN
Paperback: 978-3-7469-6194-1
Hardcover: 978-3-7469-6195-8
e-Book: 978-3-7469-6196-5

Ideal

How I wish one could amend,
T'would prove needless to repent;
All one's deeds free from dismay,
The mind content ev'ry day.

It is not to be adored,
Only say I am unflawed;
What's done were to bring on harm,
As well cut off mine own arm.

There, my foibles and false moves
Won't forsake, to me they fuse;
And words, as soon as revealed
Can, not ever, be repealed.

How to make oneself at home
With oneself? It must be known!
I should duly turn recluse,
In my exile write and muse.

Not Me

He looks at her,

He speaks to her,

Goes for walks with her;

Her hand in his,

How jammy that is!

But she

Is not me.

Her sight to me is injury,

Within, indignant mutiny,

Rust I unrelentingly

Yet shut it be inside;

This plight

Is not right.

My mind entirely worn

From the smarting it has borne

And spirit unprettily stained;

In giving I strained,

All profit now be mine;

Will he, one sweet morn,

Divine

His own twine?

Only Friend

Now they've left you one and all
And at last you've reached nightfall;
If you keep me by your side,
Courage never shall be tried.

Anguish, gloom, despair make grow
My desire not to go;
No one alone an island, true:
Thus I'll share this isle with you.

Few demands I'd surely make,
An ounce of room I'd merely take;
Boundless my devotion yet,
All my time and care you'll get.

Whate'er good will people do?
They deceive and misconstrue!
My name is loneliness and
I am the one, your only friend.

Suddenly

My tread, bewildered, on this path
Attend I passing's aftermath;

Sun that smiles, her beams fan out –
Pray what is there to smile about?

For one discovers there's a change
In mortality that's too strange.

Feelings, nature, gave plenty spark –
Suddenly, lights of life go dark;

When surging air once brought content –
Suddenly final breath be spent,

And how come a man full grown
Suddenly fits into an urn?

Distant age from here seemed so sure,

But suddenly you were no more.

Speak To Me Not Of Love

Speak to me not of love,
Tormenting, grievous thing,
For maimed and harmed am I
By its cruel deadly sting.

What parasite, what leech,
So bleed it does me dry;
How reckless, careless and
Scheming, cunning, sly.

Praised its name most warmly,
But wherefore could that be
When love has only slight
And bitterness for me?

Charmed me once – lost all spark,
No longer am I swayed;
Rouse the flame not again,
Instead I let it fade.

Down the mire goes the fort,

'Tis futile thus to build;

Speak to me not of love –

Now let these words be stilled.

Easter Sunday *

Am I nothing but a pawn
In this contest staged by fortune?
Whose favour does me o'erlook,
Rule not myself in life's forum.

Truly meagre is my gift;
Parched, this garden gone to ruin
And my weakness does but prove
To bear my load is vain doing.

Much derision do I meet,
So go to ground is my answer;
All the moments lived and lost,
Time unlived I should grieve after.

Are You near? Then as a tree,
Standing by some lake or river,
Yielding sweetest fare, I'm made,
Verdant, let me flourish ever.

* Verse 4: Adapted from Psalm 1

I Should Have Said

Feelings and words, stranded in our hearts,
And locked in they do remain;
Destined, surely not belatedly,
For expression time again.

Wealth of thoughts, not now and never said;
All intentions, worthy, kind
And how fond we were of so-and-so
Get, ungiven, left behind.

Let it be proclaimed without delay
Into perpetuity;
So the soul of dearest departed
And my voice find unity.

Hours and years are minutes and days,
Obscure all mileposts nearing;
Wait not for that occasion that might
Or might not be appearing.

If Only the Morning Would Never Come *

If only the morning would never come,
Strive and toil would find soft ending;
Leave behind the cares, the fear,
Let the rest to them be tending.

Could I find comfort in some other life,
A friend who knows a quiet space,
Where to dwell and spend time dreaming,
Sound in my good angel's embrace?

Alas! The here and now wants such kindness;
Then might not death be more forgiving?
If only the morning would never come,
It would spare me the pain of living.

* The title is a line from N.C. Hunter's play
'Waters of the Moon'

Welcome To Heaven

'So let me begin

By presenting the hereafter

To which you now have come,

Wherever it was from

And the hardships you were in –

They do not signify.

You will soon adjust,

To those residing here you can entrust

Much guidance.'

While they, permanent and practiced,

Watch in silence

And quite remember

The day they entered ...

As will we all

Awake in Arcadia,

Whatsoever our kin or kindred;

None here has fashioned a wall

Midway erstwhile tongue or hue;

Disharmony we lately knew

Now well and truly ended.

Of one flesh and blood

Are we after all;

The same bones and mud

In the end when we made it

To this heavenly hall.

Fake

In this house she moves,

Turning all to glacial,

But only superficial;

Is her flair for being nice

Conceited air instead?

She is cold as South Pole ice.

Withering her breath;

Pity them that with her live

Such as I (And why do I?),

And why this creature so uptight?

Her commands are not my wish,

How twisted it all is.

Dear me!

Human kind

She can never be!

The Customer Is King!

The way you speak, boorish, vile –
Makes my ears ever so ring;
You say I lie yet I bow,
For the customer is king!

Bicker much and rage you do,
Like a toddling little thing;
But your tantrums I must bear,
For the customer is king!

Ever pleasantly converse,
The exhaustion it does bring;
Through the hours I will crawl,
For the customer is king!

Look Inside, Dear *

Look inside, dear
Do you not see?
In your good heart,
There grows a tree.

Blossoms much dance,
Sweets that season;
Astral gath'rings
Have bright reason.

The stem, in faith,
Well found its bed;
Share crown and crest,
Symphonic tread.

In tune I am
To softly speak
Of spells and charms,
The kind you seek.

Hearts in a course

Go all around,

Were set alight;

So leap and bound.

From mast to post,

Right freshly green,

In ample style

About the scene.

Recall to mind

The ruffled strands;

So swift on foot,

Skimming the lands.

Your face speaks of

Admiration;

Look inside, dear,

There beats passion.

* Adapted from 'The Two Trees' by William
Butler Yeats, Part I

Garden Of A Dream *

Through a gate I go
On this not-too-sunny day,
With the mildest breeze,
Ev'ry hue and scent at play.

Full vegetation,
The world with its collection,
Overflowing space,
Yielding warmest expression.

The finest dwelling,
It lifts and sweetens my soul,
Charms early and late,
This Eden through which I stroll.

One and only keep,
I heed it, so it does me,
A flower as gift
Or simply stay still and see.

Image of my heart

And all the clamour its beat,

Now whisper, then roar,

Draws me thus into retreat.

Pining to be there

That which in life like a beam;

Alas! in the end,

T'was the garden of a dream.

* 'It was the garden of a dream', Leaves in the
Wind, Alpha of the Plough

Lacrimosa

Is it possible to cry for oneself?
By that mean:
Is one allowed?

Those tears convene,
At times they just do –
Liquid crowd.

No cause for unease,
Sorrow will not taint, it is well
Out of view.

Leave me to my shell;
Let me, let me
Play pitiful reprise.

The Day So Long

Yet another call
And countless emails want replies;
Ever merry greeting
For them, but my soul it dies.

Outward all is bright
While in here the blackest gloom;
I go in and grieve,
But late skip out this curséd room.

Time crawls on all fours,
Ev'ry minute a milestone stands;
Workday's end so far –
Please come, hurry! Flow, you sands!

When finally done,
It starts again tomorrow;
As I toil and grind,
The more discouraged I grow.

If you were not missed,

T'would be easier to bear,

Or I'd touch your shore –

Oh so much my life made fair!

Shadow

Why you – here with me,

I wonder?

Wouldn't you rather be

Someplace yonder?

No, she's dragged along

Instead;

Her grip is too strong,

Guarding your tread;

Perhaps you don't –

But I discern

She's near –

Your shadow.

You've yet to learn,

To me it's clear;

Entangled

Still in her net;

Rattles your cage,

There's grounds to fret;

You're at this stage,

In waters deep;

Why do you keep

Hers? get your own

Shadow.

You Are Immortal

You still move after all these years,
Sprightly making the scene as I watch;
Bright-eyed spark full to the brim –
To think you've long reached eternal lodge.

On this old tape you sing or say,
Caught my admiring ear and held it;
Preserved in some place, safe and sound,
Have me to former times connected.

In agéd light you comely stand,
A treasured photo does truly give
The sense as if time had been stayed –
Passed years ago but for me you live.

Bring Me Evening

When off to tread the mill,
I have scorn the most
For first light and next,
The day at greatest boast.

So give chase to noon,
Make it yield its powers;
But come ev'ning soon:
I shall love your hours.

The day much dictates,
With cold, crushing strain;
Let e'entide attend,
Folk turn mild again.

Captive

The full ensemble in fate's play,

None but the urban kind portray;

On track I might be underground,

In wind-swept burrows my daily round;

Then constructions, very monstrous,

Which quite offend and confound us,

Much like a fence I cannot breach,

Deadly fumes, frightful sounds besiege;

To waking, dreaming I'm confined,

In long metropolitan grind.

Where is the garden to attend,

For some herbs and flowers contend?

Not for me harvest's elation,

How rejoice at earth's creation?

The sweet crackle of frosted field,

And soft, white snow under my feet;

These I miss besides long rambles,

Catch a river's rippling mumbles,

Hear our feathered friends' symphony,

Oh nature and its rhapsody!

I Cannot Forget

What fortune it must be

Not to drudge through one's waking hours,

But time spent in pursuit,

Harmonious with a person's powers.

Indeed, there was a time

When I kept to my one-roomed castle,

Writing in tranquil state,

Away from stress and commuters' hassle.

Not a day has passed since,

That I prayed for such freedom again;

I cannot quite forget,

My calling only had to maintain.

Heart And Soul

Heart and soul in silence suffer,
While outside it must not show
In this foolish, frenzied pageant;
Grief and hurt they never know.

Bullied as one is near daily,
Keeping countless ships afloat;
After endless uphill battle,
Then keeps step on same household note.

Thus we race; where to I wonder?
But no running shoes for me;
More of easeful contemplation,
Heart and soul yet in stillness be.

Will You Ever Know?

Each day I spy you from afar,
I'm so far distant you can't see me;
And thus to meet my number one
I daydream the fates to that agree –
Will it ever be?

These heart strings of mine much playing,
Airing sighs and quavers none too few;
My polestar, only light that shines,
Place of pilgrimage I would go to –
What I feel for you.

To break my silence instantly,
But from what place should my courage flow,
And why should I be far away,
How this adoration of mine show –
Will you ever know?

Time

When nothing but

Brittle winter of life awaits,

And one by one

Memory's roads are shut,

Yet for some

It will prove

They'll not forget wretched fates,

Branches of kin, and chums

It does remove,

E'er onwards with stride

Naught but scorn would show –

Time is on our side?

Not so!

The World Inside

I live in my world inside,
T'is the most handsome shelter;
Plenty vast and cosy rooms,
Each thought a happy dweller.

Society's mob does crush,
Drains out all life and feeling;
As things go, me a stranger
The world inside e'er seeking.

Where Are They?

Katherine Mansfield , Journal entry 'Brother',
Bandol, France, November 1915

So I conclude

After many days

My mortal journey

Turned cold in the haze.

Yet could not perceive

Up to that moment

When my dearest kin

His life had broken.

While he fades away

Deep in a French grove

And I stand thus far,

Likewise boldly rove.

With the sun's embrace

Meeting deep blue breeze,

Much like his, I feel

My being did cease.

Whether this instant

Or what is in store

Fulfil no purpose

All and ever more.

Unremarkable

Now is humankind;

To venture whither

I not have a mind.

Whate'er to me worth

Is but a memoir

Of scenes and turns with

Him living they are.

'Do you remember,

Katie?' – thus he speaks

Through balm, leaf, bloom,
Dim or brightened creeks.

Has anybody,
Beside those distant,
Been to my reason
At all existent?

They, wasting, waning,
Have they ever done?
For room in this world
I allowed them none.

Poised, should I perish,
Handling… well, it cuts;
Ask if anything
Change this likely does –

Naught. – Haven't I cause
To quieten life?
But my pledge endures

When us two did thrive.

I wish (he did too)

Its author to be,

We so considered

High above the street.

Thus I spoke, it goes

On the cover clear,

This caption to him,

His name will be here.

Heaven's breath is stilled

As evening falls;

A crescent hovers,

All murmur it stalls.

From a place nearby

Hark! A woman's song,

Softly, by the stove

With a fire strong.

A humble dwelling,

Blooming clusters fine

'Neath the window and

Snug sheaf I divine.

Feathered flock settled

So like clouds of fleece;

Equine soul, sheltered,

Blanketed, at peace.

In his den the dog

Stretched out, resting head

By the woman's side,

Kitty calmly does wait.

And there's a fellow,

Yet more of a lad,

Nearing, quite unseen,

Rings his mounting tread.

But then he perceives

One bright window there,

His step much quickens,

A tune in the air.

And so, in what place

Can they now be found –

Earthlings, abiding,

Winsome all and sound?

Ringlets don't make them

Love sum of wisdom,

Not any perfect

Or pious vision.

Worthy though and fair

As long as the day,

Certainly living

And yet: Where are they?

The Dead Child

Tired world brings the night,

And night brings a dream;

I'll bring you forth again

But with morning light

Of all fantasies does drain,

You are extinguished too;

Much deceived am I –

United we'd be and true;

By morning yet

You are dead.

Saturday Again

With dismay I start the week:
Monday dawns but much too bleak;
Tuesday also does oppress,
Even if a little less;
Wednesday only halfway through
When I waken just as blue;
Edge of shadows faint in sight,
Thursday brings at last some light;
Plead when Friday's bell does chime:
How I'll make it one more time?
Sunday rises bright and clear,
Yet with dusk I'm seized by fear;
There's a space when I be sane:
Give me Saturday again.

Sospiri

(Edward Elgar)

I send my sighs into the night,
For day will not have them;
Thus as the sun descends,
Sobbing begins at dying of light
And pearly moon attends.

They sail across placid sea,
Into breakers, surging, crashing;
The trees, with whom I bide,
Sway and sigh with me –
Meadow whispers much alike.

What Was I?

How we find once in a while
Our presence here so trivial;
If we should e'er go astray,
Will they grieve at our burial?

We go forth, drop out of sight,
Turning into ash or decayed;
By all things and people shunned
Till from their memory we fade.

This cosmic giant, we learn,
It will onward storm as before,
And to all appearances
It knows of us no less, no more.

Paths and thoroughfares make din,
Eager, steady, e'er without end
In cheery, drunken shindig,
No caring thought on us do spend.

Our space not inhabited
In the worldly hall of portraits
Is by, the latest, tea time
Of none or other importance.

Perhaps consider briefly
Alive we were the other day
And next attend to business,
That whisper of ours gone astray.

In sorrow post-mid-day meal,
Still charmed by others all the same,
Yet wheel of wealth keeps turning,
Oust the fly on it we became.

But a fleeing hint on show,
Winter's diamond on water fades;
Breath turning out here and now,
For always destined to the shades.

Final darkness closing in,
Drown we will, the while they construe
Memories, slighting or fond
And ere long we fall out of view.

Heed that speckled creature's song
Rejoice at shining break of day,
Tells how flying, breathing world
Pays no mind to those gone away.

Word of springtime in its call,
Early flowers are on display,
Beeches got their tawny hue,
Morning bird on skyward parade.

What delight there used to be
In creation's rousing splendour;
A spell when all was unveiled
Appears much hopeful and tender.

In times gone by this I shared,

Onward the fair today does go,

Unaware, most marvellously,

No more am I than afterglow.

Stretched out in darkest shadows –

Everyone continues just fine

And does plainly not miss me;

Knowing I left – they give no sign.

Not trace nor residue,

So what was I to you?

Prize they do gold and gem

But what was I to them?

My name they'll not recall,

What was I after all?

'Variations on an old theme IV', Leaves in the
Wind, Alpha of the Plough

There Ain't No Fog!

There is a rumour going around
As to fog still here in London Town;
So they believe much ardently –
Such ignorance disheartens me.

Certainly a lot in days of yore
The multitude could scarcely see;
Factory chimneys in the East End
And in town to a high degree

Heaving, spewing grimy, coal-black smoke,
It mingled with the river's haze,
Made that London Particular,
That Peasouper dark nights and days.

So let us hold it with the truth,
See for yourself, behold the proof;
You might lay those delusions down –
There ain't no fog in London Town!

Another Day

Cool morning comes,
But noon and after
Burst countless suns.

So much to do:
Words in mind and books
Form patient queue.

Vacant pages,
Uncharted visions,
Tunes mere traces.

Time chiefly spent –
Squandered on chores that
Bring discontent.

The sun now sets
On another day
Filled with regrets.

Lemonade In The Shade

Journeying from
Another day of slog,
Bone-weary numb;
I saw them yonder –
Three little girls
On a patch of green;
What they were doing
Made me ponder,
The like I haven't seen;
Small table and two chairs,
A jug and plastic cups
Stood in the shade;
People walking past,
And I came along –
One of them asked,
'Would you like some lemonade?'
Present she did
A piece of paper,
What it said

I'll never know,

For I moved on;

'Although,' musing later,

'Had I bought some instead?

Certainly shall tomorrow.'

But then next eventide

They were not there,

Table and chairs abide;

Oh, what unhappy regret!

For those three girls

Were never seen again.

So Many

I have so many hopes
But more than that, fears;
Grant a sound, hearty life
Of calm umpteen years.

Let me not go under
While unversed, untried,
Before all schemes and plans
Done and laid aside.

But a house and garden,
Pleasing things within,
Whilst out sage and roses,
Trees and everything.

I have no wish to keep
In this dreary place;
So many times still dream
I'd gain a state of grace.

Weekend

There I wake from sleep elated,
Smile into the morning light;
Get up I "can", for once not "must",
Each room to me winsome bright.

Those voices from the radio
Have a much more cheery sound;
The sun or if it were to rain
And skies with beauty abound.

With appetite I start the day,
Onward time careers and hums
By far too speedily, for Oh!
Woe is me when Monday comes!

Books, Glorious Books

Indulgent champion and chum am I

Of none but books;

Why else give up my pay,

My nights, my space for them;

Only regard their brainy looks,

Take in paper-printed scent;

Mine daily bread and cuppa,

With each one I grow more content;

In all places they must be

And for every circumstance,

Be it on the go or in the smallest room,

A bedtime story;

All my knowledge they advance,

Mortals need not assume,

Besides, those pages more soul possess;

So with them I stay, surrounding me,

To keep most faithful company.

Rumination

'Impromptu for Strings', Jean Sibelius

My wings I do so want
To unfurl and stretch,
For circumstances daunt
Me sorrowful wretch.

I'd fly and see the world,
From far up above,
And down below there swirl
Games I do not love.

I'd not be near the ground
With all flaming greed,
Where cruelties abound,
These at last recede.

Lift up and carry off
That is noble, true;

Much the foolsters' loss
But only my due.

As company the winds,
Ever with me roam;
Up high where peace begins,
Softly reach I home.

Justify

On these forms you will disclose
What kind of existence you chose;
We'll check our records to see
If a winner or loser be.

Tell us that you earn a lot,
Have properties, plenty of plot;
We do hope you know the means
To tax-evade and save your beans.

'Tis the only way to prove
Your worth in this world where you move;
If strapped you're not welcome in,
Poverty is a dreadful sin!

Better make strides all the same,
You've only got yourself to blame;
Take good care there's nothing missed,
We'll let you know if you exist.

Morning Moon

On my way at early bright,
When summer's near retiring;
A firmament with its hue,
There the sun hangs admiring.

Cool breath of air even then,
I glimpsed it white and faded,
With a little time to spare
I stood and gazed and waited.

A half-moon perched there on high
In the time of its dimming;
Still the yellow star its light
In ample measure giving.

Nature

Oh I well remember
Trees at times so tall,
They to each other bow
And would sigh or call.

Wild flowers I would pick,
Gath'ring nature's store;
Mushrooms in September
Found on forest's floor.

To gaze on lush meadow,
Catch the scent of wood:
These and love for letters
Ever do me good.

Out Of Hell

Out of hell

I step into heaven:

Your room.

From this world,

Shun human company

But yours.

A shelter,

Where I finally found

My soul.

Paper

How uncomplaining you are
To ever bear my sorrows;
Of these a great many in
All todays and tomorrows.

Notebook, journal, diary,
Loyal comrade, helpmeet, mate:
Paper for my heart-to-heart,
They unconditionally wait.

Capricious mortals hasten,
Barely heed souls in despair;
Still you welcome my wishes
And pleas my pen wants to share.

Rainy Day Reflections

How I wish it were not this way,
Dreary toiling ev'ry day,
Ever jaded, frayed;
Hardly time of my very own,
Pennies – just – gained from grindstone,
And how soon they fade!

Break of day too dismal to bear,
Rising with dread and despair,
But go on I must;
May these wheels carry me back home
Instead in e'er rolling tomb
To business be rushed.

Days, weeks come and fly, all squandered,
Yet much ground left unconquered,
Nothing to reveal;
Blossoms burgeon, ere long they wilt,
Leaves burst out and then be spilt,

Never-ending wheel.

Seasons enter to leave again,

They may shine on me or rain,

I'll only wither;

When at last will my heart be glad,

And a decent life be had,

Fortune draw hither?

Robber! Thief!

Without warning you broke in,

Invading body and mind;

Struck me smartly on the head,

Left devastation behind.

You took off with all my goods

And my dignity besides;

Is it a challenge to fight

Or how best to traumatise?

I did not invite you in –

How crass of you to intrude!

Take all malady from here

And thus grant me solitude.

Qualities

My good will to gain
And kindly favour,
A man must surely have
Ways with not a stain,
Be wise and clever.

One in whom I can trust,
About all living things does care,
Shows courage, ever just;
Alas! suchlike virtues prove rare.

Do Not Worry

'Mach dir keine Sorgen', Marlen Haushofer

Do not worry, for you have seen
Too little and too much,
As any of our human kind
Before you weathered such.

The tears you have shed, aplenty,
Or not enough, who knows?
As up to now the selfsame for
Everybody goes.

You've had bountiful affection,
Aversion just the same,
Near two decades; what do they mean
In this here living game?

And so you quite gave up living,
In every way did them

Who found they'd not ever go on
To love or hate again.

The anguish you have long suffered,
Not willingly – who does?
Your body soon got burdensome,
Love for it there never was.

How unfortunate, then again,
The opposite could meet,
For from a body so unloved
The soul swiftly would fleet.

What about the soul, can you tell
You've ever one possessed?
Whereas it seems reason only,
Which feelings ne'er addressed.

Or have you been moved now and then,
If for a little while,
When you beheld summer's flower,

Feline eyes did beguile?

The anguish over someone's fate

Or statue, tree and stone,

Those truly agile, fork-tailed birds

Swoop and dart over Rome?

Do not worry, for even if

A soul had lived within,

Longest slumber its greatest wish,

Gone all physical pain.

Priceless sap of life, tissue, cells,

Nought but cinders one day;

Thoughts at last stand still – God be thanked,

If He's more than hearsay.

Your sad lot will have been in vain,

Do not worry – 'tis so;

Each and all have had to face it,

One more story does show.

Zeitfracht Medien GmbH
Ferdinand-Jühlke-Straße 7
99095 Erfurt, Deutschland
produktsicherheit@kolibri360.de